DATE DUE

NOV 3 0 2005

DEMCO 38-296

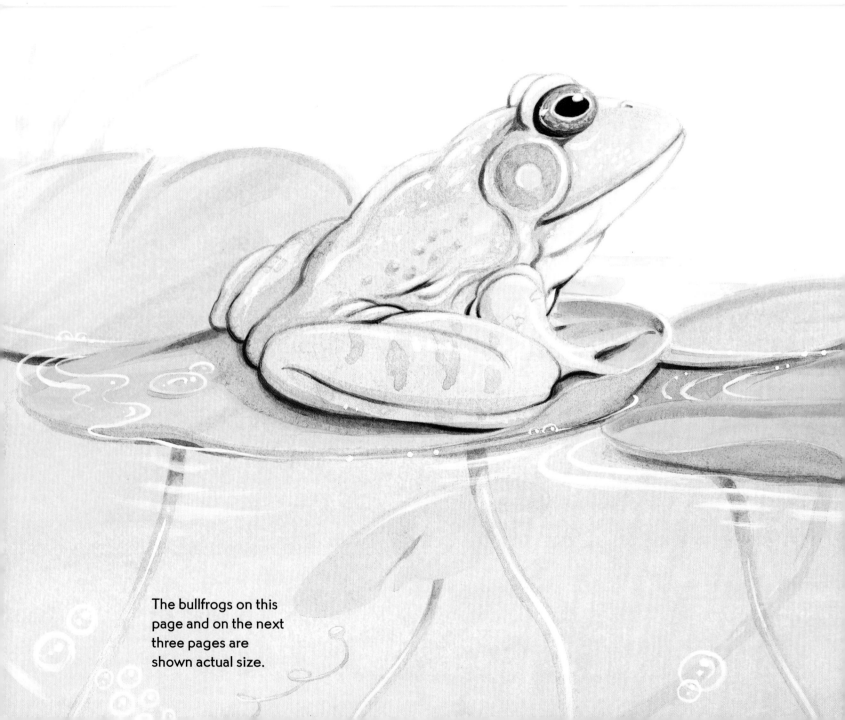

The bullfrogs on this page and on the next three pages are shown actual size.

ALL ABOUT FROGS

JIM ARNOSKY

Scholastic Press • New York

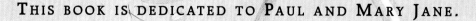

THIS BOOK IS DEDICATED TO PAUL AND MARY JANE.

Library of Congress Cataloging-in-Publication Data
Arnosky, Jim.
All about frogs / Jim Arnosky   p. cm.
1. Frogs—Juvenile literature. [1. Frogs.] I. Title.   QL668.E2 A68 2002   597.8'9—dc21   2001020680
ISBN 0-590-48164-9
10 9 8 7 6 5 4   03 04 05 06
Printed in Singapore   46
First printing, March 2002
The text type was set in 16-point Raleigh Demi-Bold.
Jim Arnosky made these paintings using acrylic paint on acid-free watercolor paper.

Have you ever wondered about frogs?
How many kinds of frogs are there?
Where do frogs live?
What do frogs eat?
How do tadpoles change into frogs?
How big can a frog grow?
This book answers all these questions and more.
It's all about frogs.

Frogs, toads, and salamanders are amphibians. Amphibians are animals that begin life in water as tadpoles. They slowly develop limbs and lungs and eventually live primarily on land.

All amphibians are cold-blooded. They warm up in the sun and cool off in the shade. Frogs hop into the water to cool off and to keep safe from hungry predators.

bullfrog and lily pads

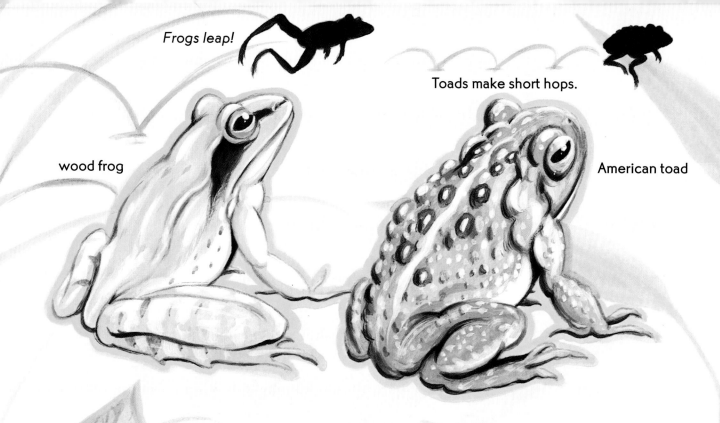

Frogs leap!

Toads make short hops.

wood frog

American toad

tree frog

Frogs and toads are similar but different animals. Frogs have moist, smooth skin. Toads have dry, bumpy skin. Frogs have large hind legs and can jump great distances. Toads have small hind legs and can only make short hops.

frog

toad

Frogs are slender in shape. Toads look fat.

Because of their jumping ability, frogs almost always try to flee from danger. Toads squat down and stay motionless. Many predators eat frogs. Few predators eat toads because when a toad is threatened its skin excretes moisture that irritates the eyes, mouth, and nasal membranes of many animals, including humans. The moisture does not, however, cause warts.

Frogs are mostly found in and around water.

Toads are commonly seen away from water.

Frogs live on every continent except Antarctica. Worldwide, there are more than one thousand species of frogs. Every one can be identified by its color and markings. Here are the most common North American frogs and their usual environments.

All of the frogs on these two pages are shown at normal adult size.

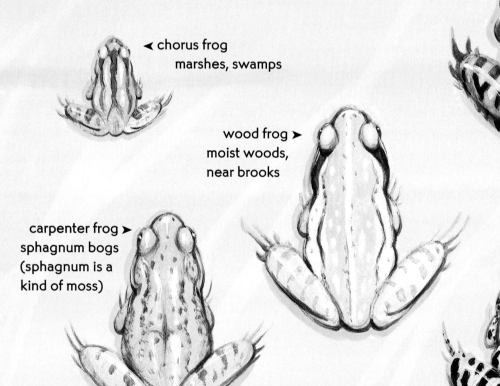

◄ pickerel frog
swamps, bogs, small streams

◄ chorus frog
marshes, swamps

wood frog ►
moist woods, near brooks

carpenter frog ►
sphagnum bogs (sphagnum is a kind of moss)

◄ crawfish frog
bayous, riverbanks

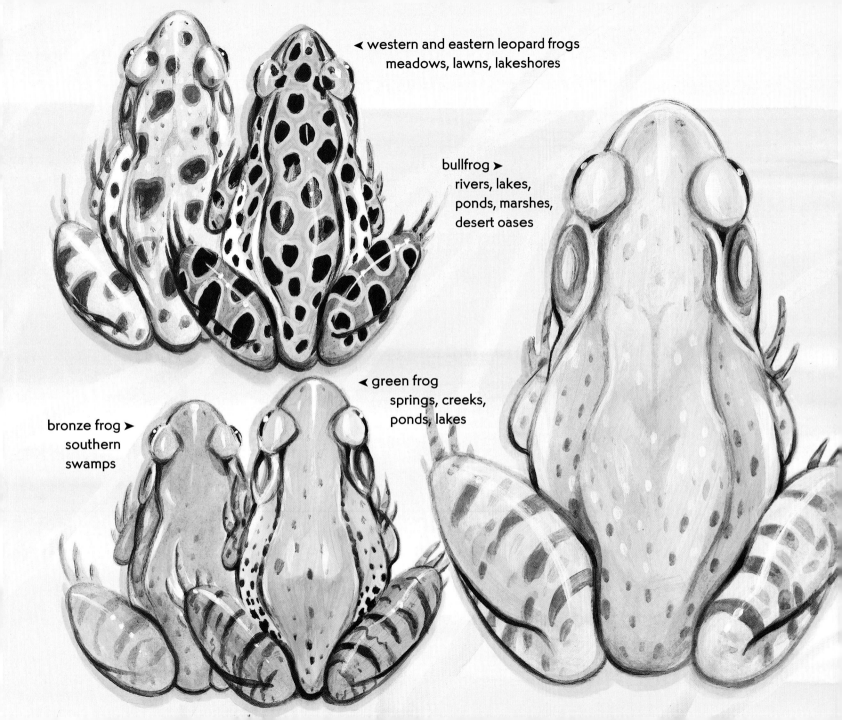

◄ western and eastern leopard frogs
meadows, lawns, lakeshores

bullfrog ➤
rivers, lakes,
ponds, marshes,
desert oases

◄ green frog
springs, creeks,
ponds, lakes

bronze frog ➤
southern
swamps

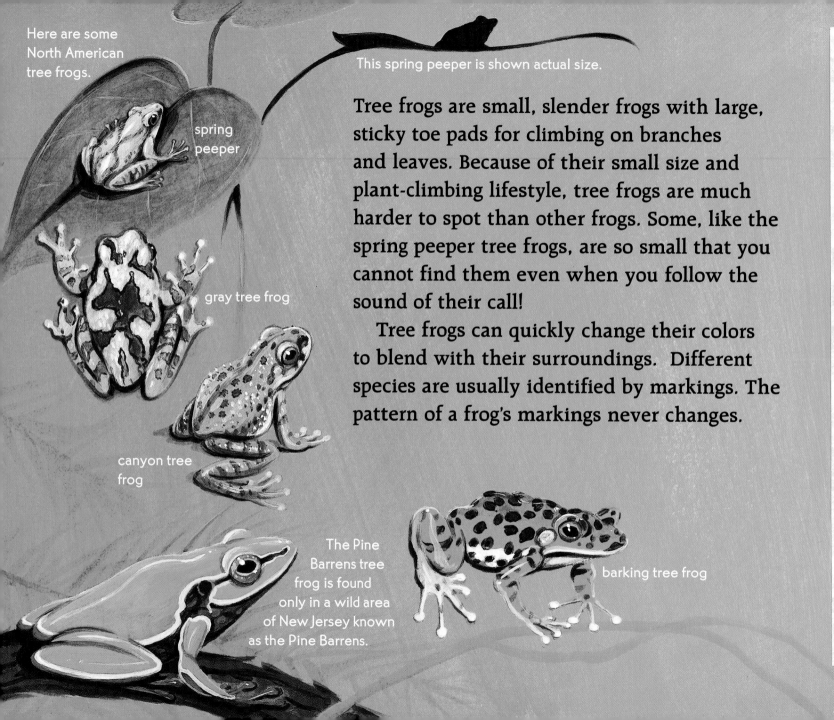

Here are some North American tree frogs.

spring peeper

This spring peeper is shown actual size.

gray tree frog

canyon tree frog

The Pine Barrens tree frog is found only in a wild area of New Jersey known as the Pine Barrens.

barking tree frog

Tree frogs are small, slender frogs with large, sticky toe pads for climbing on branches and leaves. Because of their small size and plant-climbing lifestyle, tree frogs are much harder to spot than other frogs. Some, like the spring peeper tree frogs, are so small that you cannot find them even when you follow the sound of their call!

Tree frogs can quickly change their colors to blend with their surroundings. Different species are usually identified by markings. The pattern of a frog's markings never changes.

There are more tree frogs in Central and South America than in any other place on Earth. Tree frogs living in tropical places are more brilliant in color and have bolder markings than tree frogs living anywhere else.

The spectacularly colorful tree frogs known as poison frogs excrete a poisonous fluid through their skin. Their colors and markings serve as warnings to predators: DO NOT EAT!

red-eyed tree frog

green-and-black poison frog

red-backed poison frog

golden palm tree frog

dyeing poison frog (dyeing is the species name)

A frog's squatting position, with all limbs tucked in, conserves moisture.

A frog's body is mostly skin and muscle on a small skeleton. A frog's most powerful muscles are its leg muscles and the muscle that rapidly thrusts its tongue out to snap up insects.

Frogs absorb moisture through their skin. The folds of skin around a frog's limbs help retain the moisture.

The base of a frog's tongue is attached at the front of its mouth. A powerful muscle flips the tongue forward.

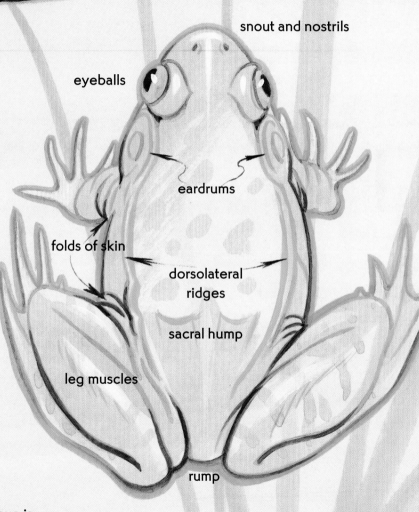

topside view of a typical frog

snout and nostrils

eyeballs

eardrums

folds of skin

dorsolateral ridges

sacral hump

leg muscles

rump

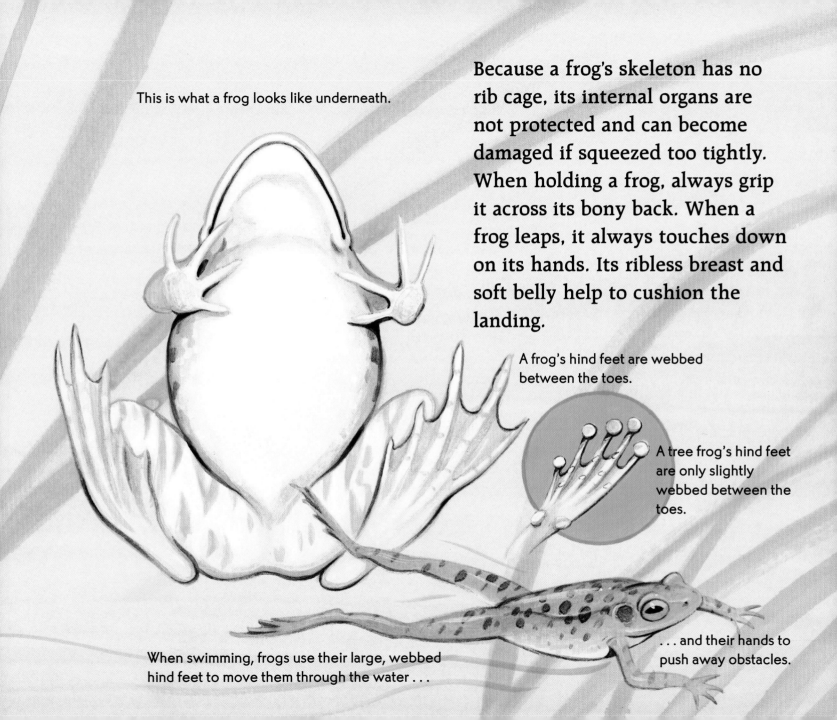

This is what a frog looks like underneath.

Because a frog's skeleton has no rib cage, its internal organs are not protected and can become damaged if squeezed too tightly. When holding a frog, always grip it across its bony back. When a frog leaps, it always touches down on its hands. Its ribless breast and soft belly help to cushion the landing.

A frog's hind feet are webbed between the toes.

A tree frog's hind feet are only slightly webbed between the toes.

When swimming, frogs use their large, webbed hind feet to move them through the water . . .

. . . and their hands to push away obstacles.

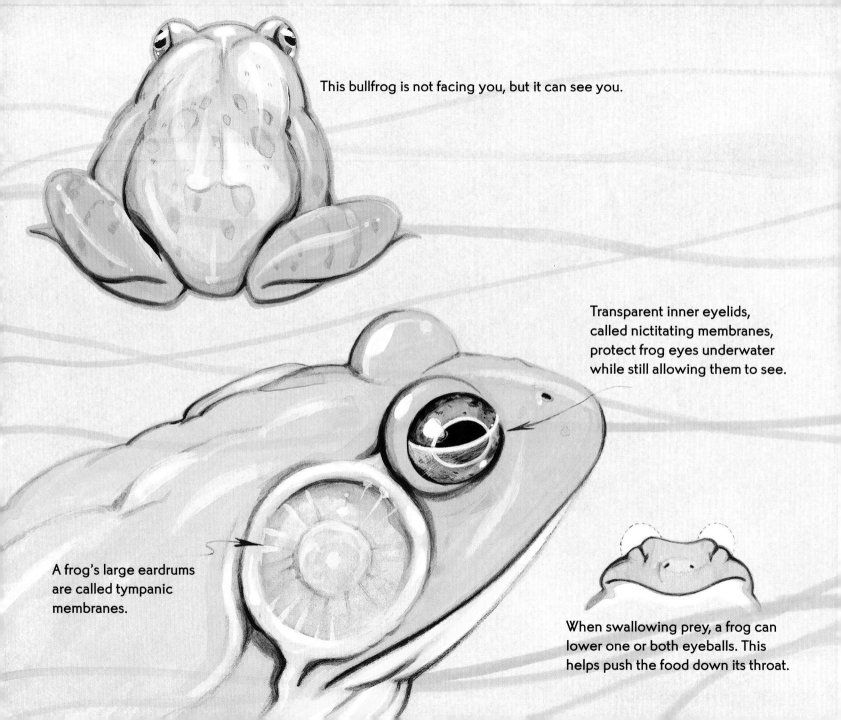

This bullfrog is not facing you, but it can see you.

Transparent inner eyelids, called nictitating membranes, protect frog eyes underwater while still allowing them to see.

A frog's large eardrums are called tympanic membranes.

When swallowing prey, a frog can lower one or both eyeballs. This helps push the food down its throat.

A frog's head is wide to accommodate a huge mouth. Frogs swallow food whole. Large external eardrums provide excellent hearing, alerting a frog to the sounds of approaching danger. And big eyeballs give a frog a 360-degree view of the world.

In many species of frogs, you can tell females from males by the size of their eardrums. If the eardrum is smaller than the eye, the frog is a female. If it is larger than the eye, the frog is a male. In every other way, male and female frogs look alike.

male mink frog

female mink frog

CLUCK CLUCK

call of the wood frog

CROAK

call of the pickerel frog

BARK

call of the barking frog

two vocal sacs inflated

Only male frogs make sounds. They call to attract female frogs. Frogs produce sounds by inflating vocal sacs in their throats and vibrating the air as they slowly let it out. Some species inflate one large vocal sac. Others inflate two small vocal sacs.

single vocal sac inflated

spring peeper calling

PEEP PEEP PEEP

call of the spring peeper

GRUNT GRUNT

call of the pig frog

PLUNK

call of the green frog

KER RRROCK

call of the leopard frog

The sound each species of frog makes when calling
is as distinctive as the species color and markings.

JUG-O-RUM

call of the bullfrog

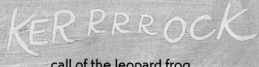

CHIRP
CHIRP
CHIRP

call of the chorus frog

TRILLLLLLLL

call of the gray tree frog

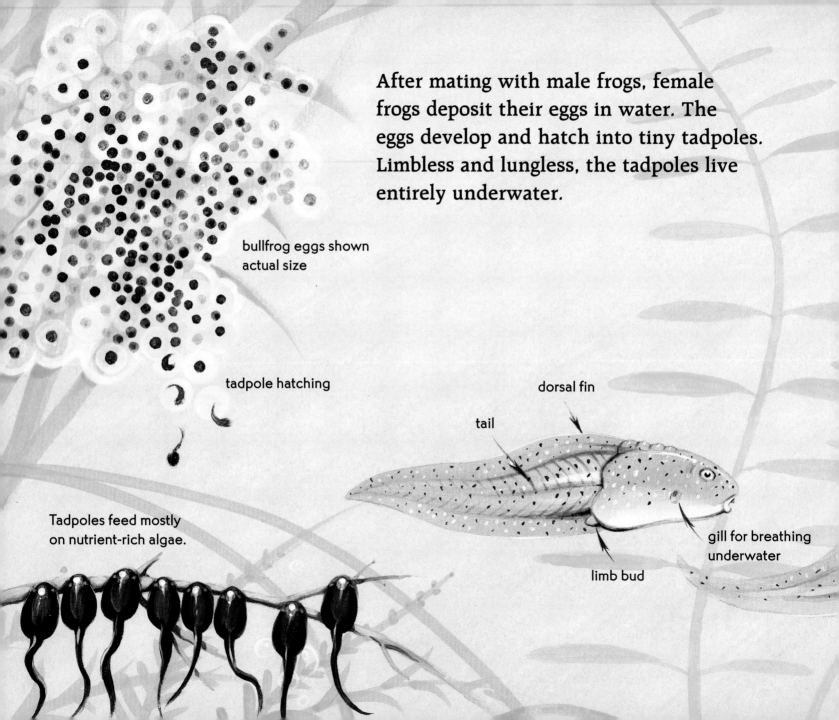

After mating with male frogs, female frogs deposit their eggs in water. The eggs develop and hatch into tiny tadpoles. Limbless and lungless, the tadpoles live entirely underwater.

bullfrog eggs shown actual size

tadpole hatching

tail

dorsal fin

gill for breathing underwater

limb bud

Tadpoles feed mostly on nutrient-rich algae.

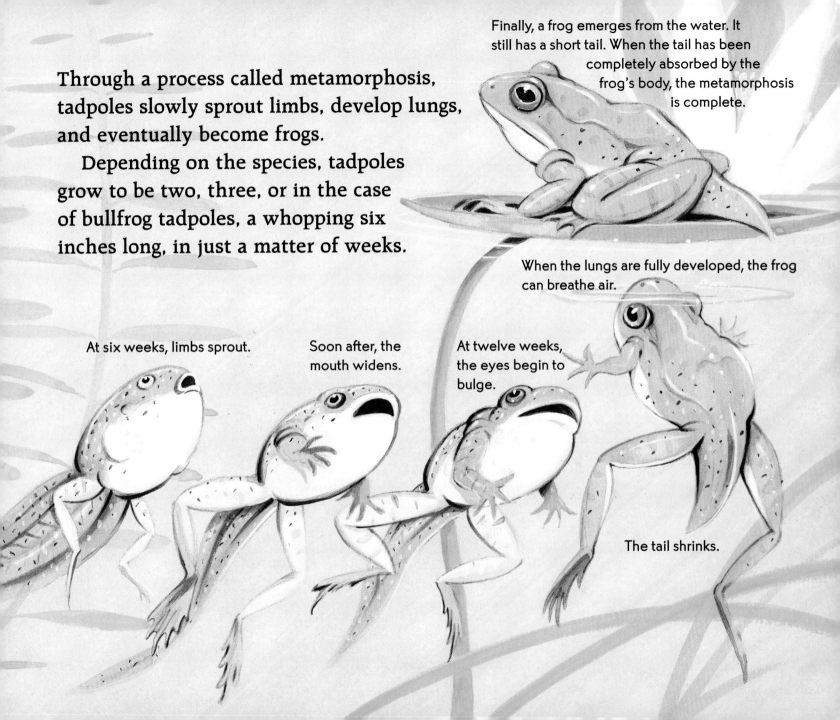

Through a process called metamorphosis, tadpoles slowly sprout limbs, develop lungs, and eventually become frogs.

Depending on the species, tadpoles grow to be two, three, or in the case of bullfrog tadpoles, a whopping six inches long, in just a matter of weeks.

Finally, a frog emerges from the water. It still has a short tail. When the tail has been completely absorbed by the frog's body, the metamorphosis is complete.

When the lungs are fully developed, the frog can breathe air.

At six weeks, limbs sprout.

Soon after, the mouth widens.

At twelve weeks, the eyes begin to bulge.

The tail shrinks.

Small and medium-size frogs eat mostly insects, which they snap up with their sticky tongues. The silhouettes on this page show some of the insects frogs eat.

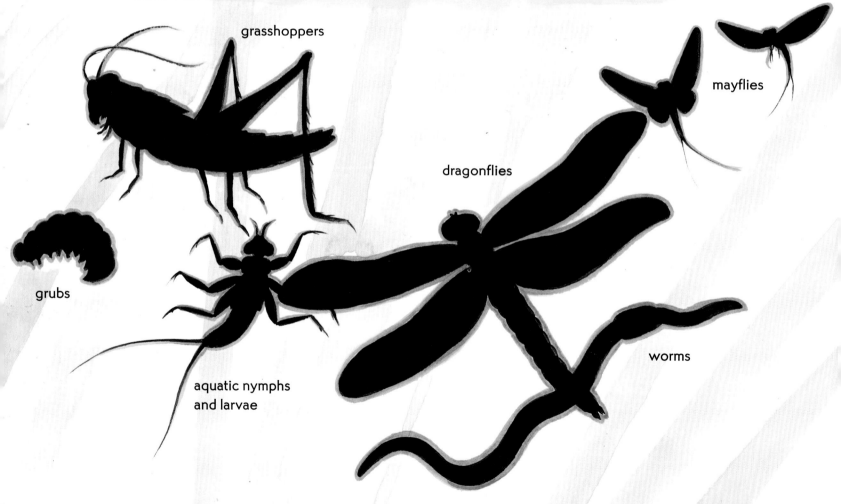

moths

grasshoppers

mayflies

dragonflies

grubs

aquatic nymphs and larvae

worms

Large frogs eat worms, small snakes, fish, mice, baby turtles, and even other frogs as well as insects. Frogs help to keep the numbers of insects down.

I once saw a great big bullfrog catch and eat two adult goldfinches. The frog swallowed the second bird almost immediately after the first! Large bullfrogs have been known to swallow ducklings whole.

All kinds of animals eat frogs. Wherever frogs live, they are hunted day and night.

So many different birds, reptiles, fish, and mammals catch and eat frogs—it is amazing that frogs survive the pressure . . .

but they do.

In the natural order of things, frogs can take care of themselves. But frogs cannot avoid or escape environmental dangers such as water pollution and the loss of wetland habitats.

Sometimes I walk along a shoreline just to count the frogs that suddenly leap into the water. I always count more frogs than I imagined I would see. That's the way I like it. That's the way it should forever be.